ANIMALS IN U.S. HISTORY

TEXAS LONGHORN

Lynn M. Stone

Rourke
Publishing LLC
Vero Beach, Florida 32964

© 2004 Rourke Publishing LLC

All rights reserved. No part of this book may be reproduced or utilized in any form or by any means, electronic or mechanical including photocopying, recording, or by any information storage and retrieval system without permission in writing from the publisher.

www.rourkepublishing.com

PHOTO CREDITS:
Cover, title page, pp. 4, 8, 10, 19, 20, 22 © Lynn M. Stone; pp. 6, 13, 16 courtesy of The Kansas State Historical Society, Topeka; pp. 7, 12, 14, 18 courtesy of Western History Collections, University of Oklahoma Libraries

Title page: *The wide horns of a long-gone longhorn lie in a nest of Texas wildflowers.*

Editor: Frank Sloan

Cover design by Nicola Stratford
Interior design by Heather Scarborough

Library of Congress Cataloging-in-Publication Data

Stone, Lynn M.
  Texas longhorn / Lynn M. Stone.
     p. cm. -- (Animals in U.S. history)
Summary: Introduces the Texas longhorn and its importance in the history of the United States.
Includes bibliographical references and index.
  ISBN 1-58952-702-X (hardcover)
  1. Texas longhorn cattle--History--Juvenile literature. [1. Texas longhorn cattle--History. 2. Cattle--History. 3. Southwest, New--History.] I. Title. II. Series: Stone, Lynn M. Animals in U.S. history.
  SF199.T48S76 2003
  636.2'8--dc21
                                        2003009730

Printed in the USA

CG/CG

COLOMA PUBLIC LIBRARY

30151000043666

DATE DUE

MR 3 1 '06			

Demco, Inc. 38-294

COLOMA PUBLIC LIBRARY

TABLE OF CONTENTS

Longhorns and the Beef Business 5

An Unusual Breed 9

The Cattle Drives 15

The Cattle Drives End 18

Longhorns Today 21

Glossary 23

Index 24

Further Reading 24

Websites to Visit 24

Longhorns and the Beef Business

Much of the American West is **beef** cattle country. Cattle graze over millions of acres of grassland. Beef cattle are a big business in the western United States.

Modern North American beef cattle come in many different **breeds**. And many cattle are a mix of breeds. But America's huge beef cattle **industry** began with just one breed, the Texas longhorn.

The Texas longhorn was named for the wide, sweeping horns worn by both bulls and cows.

The longhorn began an industry of huge importance. It also helped America grow and expand westward. Many towns grew up around the trade in longhorns.

Dodge City, Kansas, shown here in 1878, became famous because of the trade in longhorns.

Cowboys keep a herd of longhorns together on the plains of the Old West.

Like the cowboys who rounded them up, longhorns have become a **symbol** of the Old West. Without longhorns, America's beef cattle industry would have indeed grown more slowly. But the longhorn was—and remains—an unusual breed.

An Unusual Breed

The first thing anyone notices about a longhorn is, of course, its long horns. Sometimes the tips of those long, handlebar horns are 6 feet (1.8 meters) or more apart!

Longhorns are a part of their dry, western environment. They are just about as comfortable in their **environment** as cactus and sagebrush.

Longhorns can have horns wider across than the height of a grown man.

Longhorns owe their toughness to their **ancestors**. Those were Spanish cattle brought to North America in the 1500s. Many of them escaped. They lived off the rugged land, mostly in Mexico. Beginning around 1820, Texans and other ranchers mixed herds of criollo with cattle from the East.

The new cattle, the Texas longhorns, were largely of the wide-horned, Mexican criollo type. But with new **bloodlines**, they weren't as bony. The new bloodlines also gave the longhorns many colors.

Modern longhorns are bigger and more colorful than the pure Spanish cattle.

Beginning in the 1850s, new American settlements as far west as California needed fresh meat. Outside of Mexico and Texas there were few beef herds.

An old photograph shows cowboys on a cattle drive taking a break by their chuck wagon.

Cowboys with bullwhips drive longhorns in this old drawing first printed in Smalley's History of the Northern Pacific Railroad.

Furthermore, the western railroads were just being built. The only way to move cattle to the market was to drive them there.

The Cattle Drives

Texans realized there was money to be made with their beef cattle, many of them roaming wild. In 1865, for example, a longhorn was worth $4 in Texas. It was worth $30 to $40 in the North.

Cowboys on horseback began rounding up longhorns. The **mounted** cowboys drove the cattle hundreds of miles to towns east, north, or west. Some of the drives traveled 1,500 miles (2,419 kilometers)!

Frederic Remington was a famous painter of scenes of the Old West. This Remington painting shows how cowboys kept their longhorns on the move even in wintry weather.

The cattle lived off the land, as their ancestors had for 300 years. No other breed in North America could have done what the longhorns did.

Over the next 20 years or so, herds of longhorns thundered across the open grasslands. Millions of longhorns were driven to market. Their hooves kicked up clouds of dust that could be seen for miles. But the old, wild West was changing.

A drawing published in 1867 shows Colonel O.W. Wheeler's herd of longhorns reaching to the horizon.

The Cattle Drives End

By the 1880s the long cattle drives were finished. The railroads had reached many towns. Cattle did not have to be driven very far. Many Western states by now had plenty of their own cattle. And the once open grasslands were being fenced in.

By the 1880s, cattle needed to be driven only to the nearest railroad stockyards. From there the cattle were loaded into train cars and shipped to market.

Herefords were easier to load into trains because they had short horns, or no horns at all.

Longhorns were finished, too. New breeds, like British Herefords, were being raised. They weren't as tough as longhorns. They didn't dig cactus roots for snacks. They were fatter, though, and they gained weight faster.

Longhorns Today

Big ranchers gave up on Texas longhorns. A small herd was taken to Wichita Mountains National Wildlife Refuge in 1927 to help save the breed.

In the years since, however, American ranchers have taken a new interest in longhorns. Longhorns are popular again, not so much for their meat as for their looks. But they are also popular because they are truly history on the hoof.

The 1,500 true longhorns left in 1964 have increased to more than 100,000.

Glossary

ancestors (AN sess turz) — those from whom others have come into being

beef (BEEF) — the meat of cattle; the cattle breeds raised for their meat

bloodlines (BLUHD LYNZ) — types or strains of animals

breeds (BREEDZ) — particular kinds of domestic animals within a larger group of very similar animals, such as the Texas longhorn among the cattle group

environment (en VY ren ment) — one's surroundings, especially the natural surroundings like air, land, and water

industry (IN des tree) — a system in which things are built, produced, or raised

mounted (MAUNT ed) — to be on horseback

symbol (SIM bel) — a thing that stands for something, such as a flag standing for a country

Longhorns graze in Theodore R. Roosevelt National Park, North Dakota.

Index

breeds   5, 19
cattle   5, 11, 15
cattle drives   15, 18
cattle industry   5, 6, 7
cowboys   7, 15
criollo   11
Herefords   19
herds   11, 12, 17
Mexico   11, 12
Old West   7, 17
railroads   13, 18
Texas   12, 15
Wichita Mountains National Wildlife Refuge   21

Further Reading
Find out more about longhorns with these helpful books:
- Alter, Judy. *Exploring and Mapping the American West.* Children's Press, 2001.
- Stanley, Gerry. *Cowboys and Longhorns: A Portrait of the Long Drive.* Crown, 2003.
- Sundling, Charles W. *Cowboys of the Frontier.* Abdo, 2000.

Websites to Visit:
- www.texasalmanac.com/texascattle.html
- www.dfwnetmall.com/e-mag/longhorn.htm

About the Author
Lynn Stone is a talented natural history photographer and writer. Lynn, a former teacher, travels worldwide to photograph wildlife in their natural habitat. He has more than 500 children's books to his credit.